This book belongs to:

_____

Please handle with care!

In the vast ocean, where waves gently sway,
Lived Zorca, the Baby Orca, who led the way.

Orcinus orca, the scientific name to say,
A majestic mammal, ruling the ocean's sway.

His mother, Nynu, a matriarch so wise,
Her tales echo through oceanic skies.

Nynu leads the pod, in the ocean's ballet.
Covering 90 miles daily, gracefully they play.

Nynu's dorsal fin stood proud, reaching high.
6 feet of magnificence against the blue sky.

Intelligent marvel, she led with great flair.
Coordinating hunts, a captain, wow, rare.

Zorca, the young one, full of curiosity,
Yearned to explore the 7 blue seas.

He asked Nynu about orca's claim to fame,
And why they were called "such an awful
name."

"My dear Zorca," Nynu said with grace,
"Our name comes from an ancient embrace."

A bus-length in stature, a sight to behold,
Six tons of strength, as ancient stories are told.

No sense of smell, in the sea they'd dwell,
Guided by instincts, a marine life carousel.

In every ocean they roam, from Arctic to Antarctic span,
Fifty Thousand strong, a diverse orca clan.

Zorca listened intently, his heart filled with pride,
To be part of a pod of orcas totaling 55.

He learned about orcas, A culture they held, like humans do,
Dialects unique, traditions passed through.

A pod they called home, a family so tight,
Carnivores they were, with an appetite for marine delight.

Fish, squids, and crustaceans, their meals of the day,
Hunters of the deep, masters of the hunting display.

Nynu taught Zorca, lessons on breaching, Zorca, eagerly await, to learn lessons on beaching.

See each orca pod are unique, in their own way
From their dialect and culture, to socializing and play.

Nynu told Zorca of the orcas' long sleep,
A fascinating secret, so precious and deep.

For they couldn't sleep like humans do,
With one eye open, dreams they'd pursue.

Zorca leads the pod, in the Pacific ballet, Eating sharks with might, in the ocean's play.

Zorca grew older, his knowledge did grow,
A guardian of the sea, his purpose to show.

He witnessed the threats, the dangers they faced,
Commercial hunting and their homes displaced.

Nets and pollution, ships at night,
vast Oil spills, oh no such a sad sight.

Nynu's sweet songs muffled by mans might.
Zorca's pod endures, these perilous plights.

Nynu taught Zorca about breeding and birth,
The miracle of life, the wonders of Earth.

Gestation, a marvel, a lengthy affair,
Fifteen to eighteen months, a journey to
bear.

"Females give birth every few years," Nynu shared,
"To ensure that our young are properly prepared."

New calves in intervals, every three to five years.
In the rhythm of life, they'd conquer their fears.

With each passing day, Zorca's heart grew strong,
His love for the ocean, forever a song.

In the vast and endless sea, where the waves dance with glee,
Lived Zorca, the largest dolphin, from the Delphinidae family.

With clicks and whistles, they shared tales of old,
Knowledge passed down, a legacy bold.

In pods close-knit, they'd journey afar, 90 miles daily, like a twinkling star.

In the heart of the ocean, where mysteries unfold,
Zorca and his pod, a saga forever told.

Beaching on shores, a tactic so rare,
To feast on sea lions, their oceanic affair.

With each breach and dive, a story to unveil,
In the vast, endless sea, where Zorca and is
pod set sail.

The End

# Orca Fun Facts

Common name: Orca (Killer Whale)

Scientific name: Orcinus orca

Type: Mammals

Diet: Carnivore

Group name: Pod

Weight: Up to 6 tons

Size: 23 to 32 feet

Average life span in the wild: 50 to 90 years

# Pop Quiz!

Does orca whales live in all 7 seas?

How many miles can a pod of orcas travel daily?

Does orcas sleep with both eyes close?

Are all orca pods the same?

How many years can an orca live?

What is the name for a family of orcas?

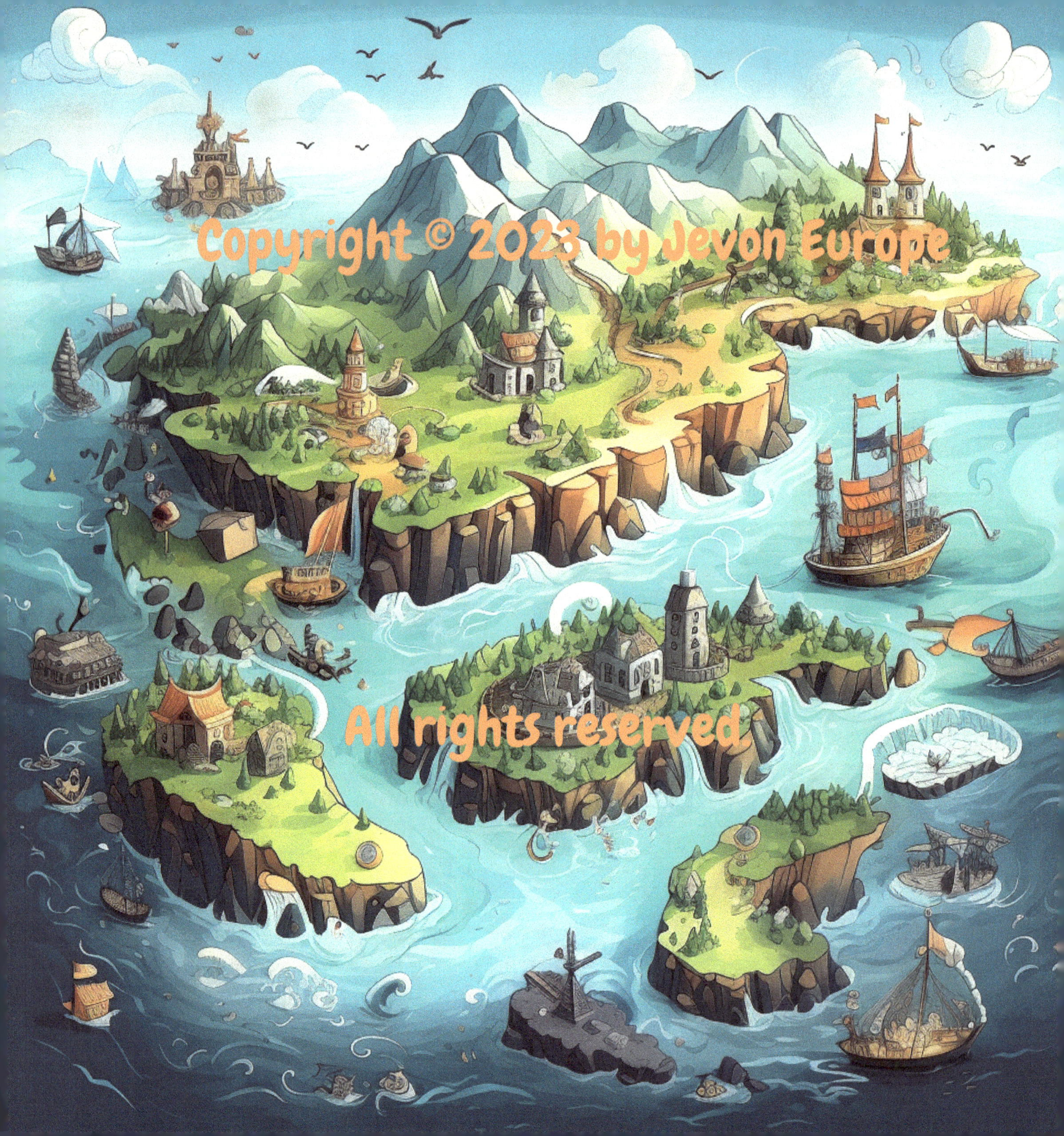